My Body is My Body

It's As Simple As Black and White

Bethany James

Little Hearts Matter, LLC
Fairfield, California

My Body is My Body: It's As Simple As Black and White Copyright © 2014 by Bethany James

All rights reserved. No part of this book may be reproduced or transmitted in any form or by any means without written permission of the author except in the case of brief quotations embodied in critical articles and reviews. For information address Little Hearts Matter, LLC at the address listed below.

ISBN 978-0-692-21286-8

Library of Congress Control Number: 2014910387

Cover by: Donna Osborn Clark at CreationsbyDonna@gmail.com

Interior designed by: interiorbookdesigns.com

Published by:

Little Hearts Matter, LLC

P.O. Box 607

Fairfield, California 94533

This Book Belongs To:

_____

(Color Me!)

This book is dedicated to my children, John, Michael, Corey, and Courtney, my grandchildren and my Little Man. And to all the parents that trusted me to care for their children in my child care home.

Special Thanks!

Special thanks to Glenda Wallace, CEO of Pink Kiss Publishing Company, for her assistance in launching this project, and Donna Osborn Clark for the amazing cover design.

My Body is My Body

It's As Simple As Black and White

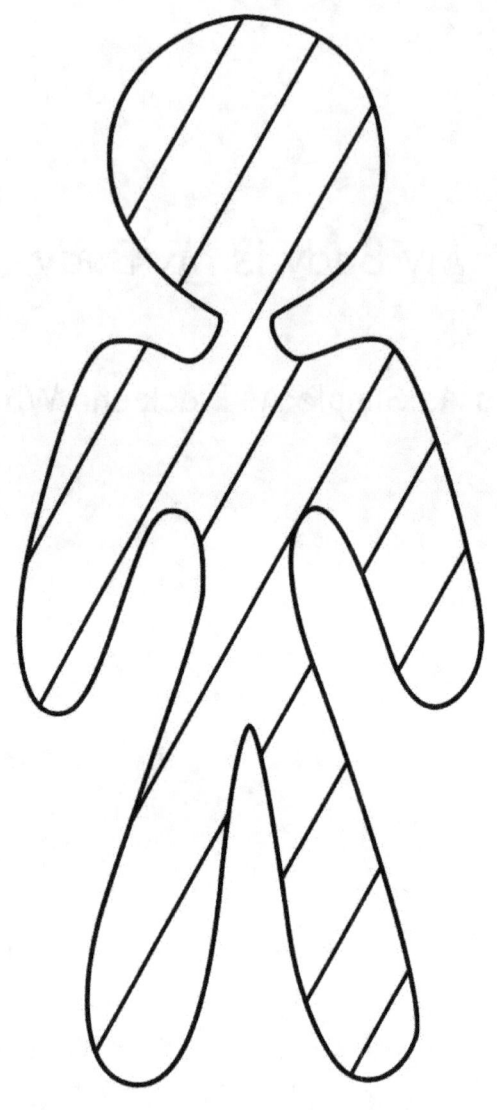

My Body is My Body.

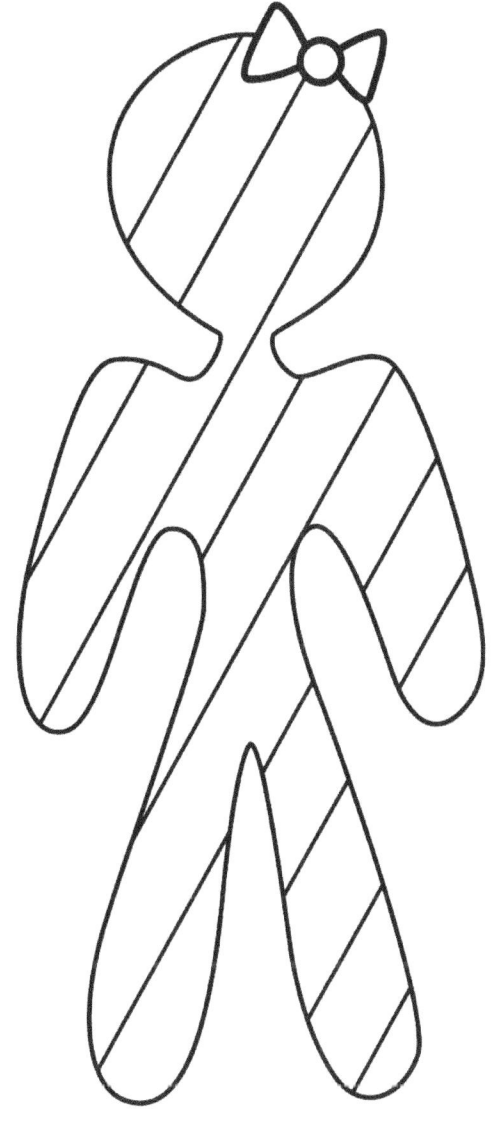

Help me keep it safe.

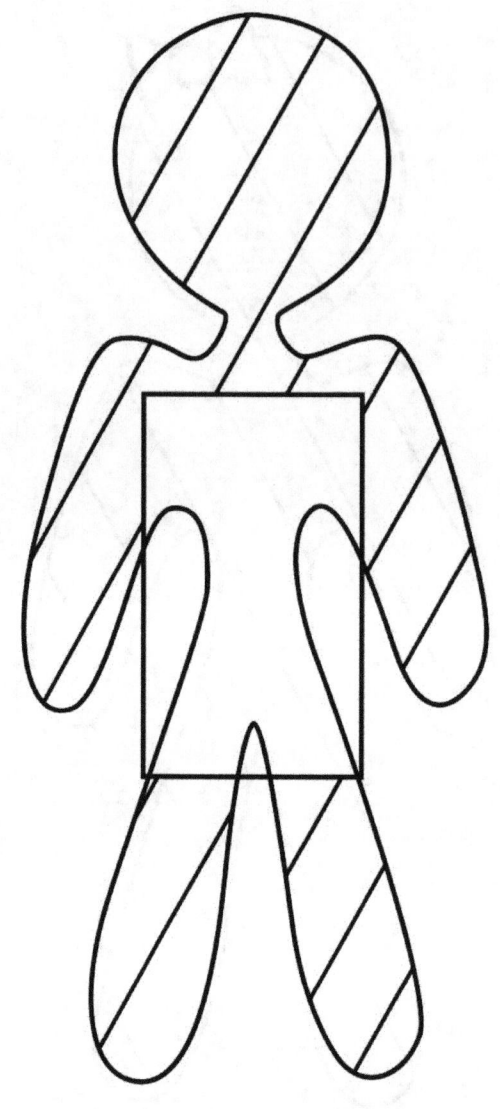

My Body is My Body.

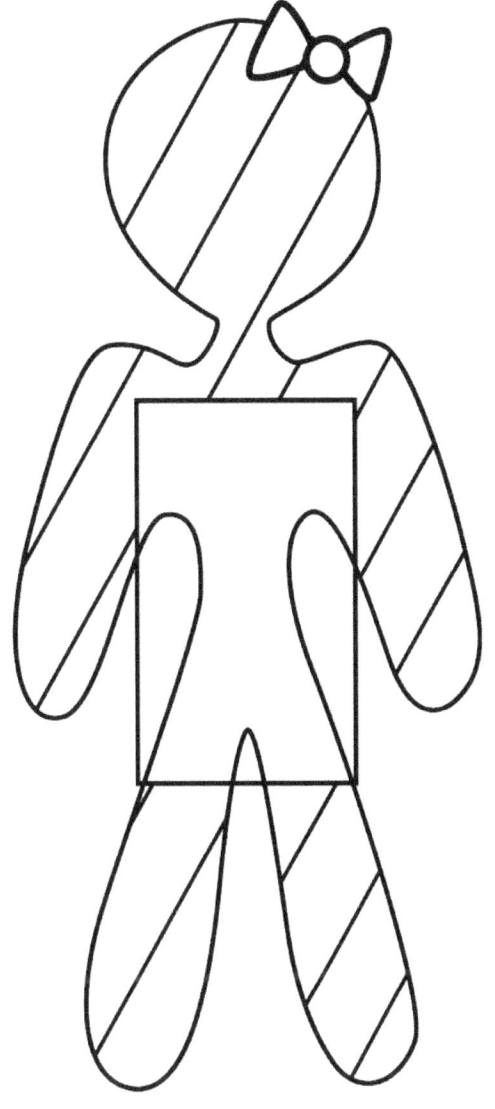

Please don't touch this place.

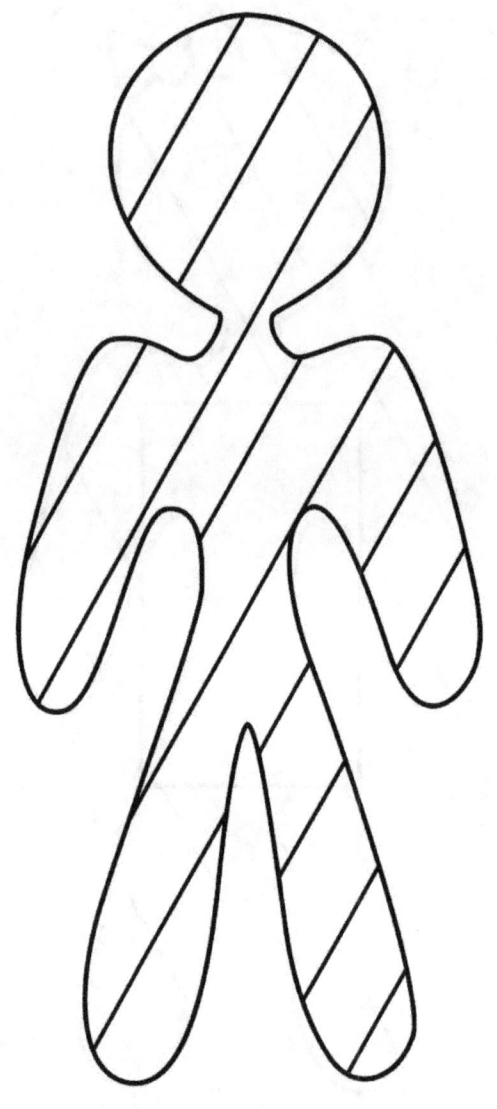

My Body is My Body.

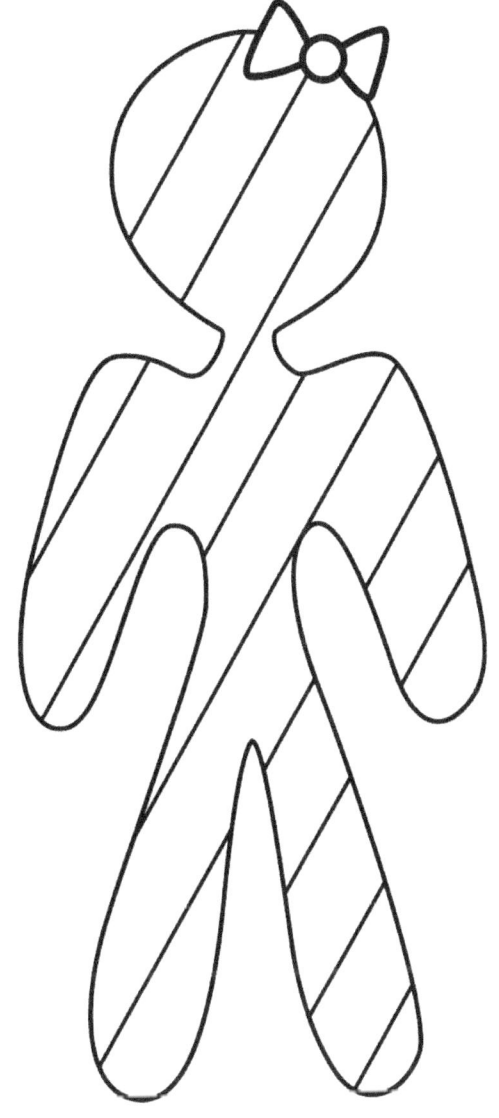

No inappropriate touching, please.

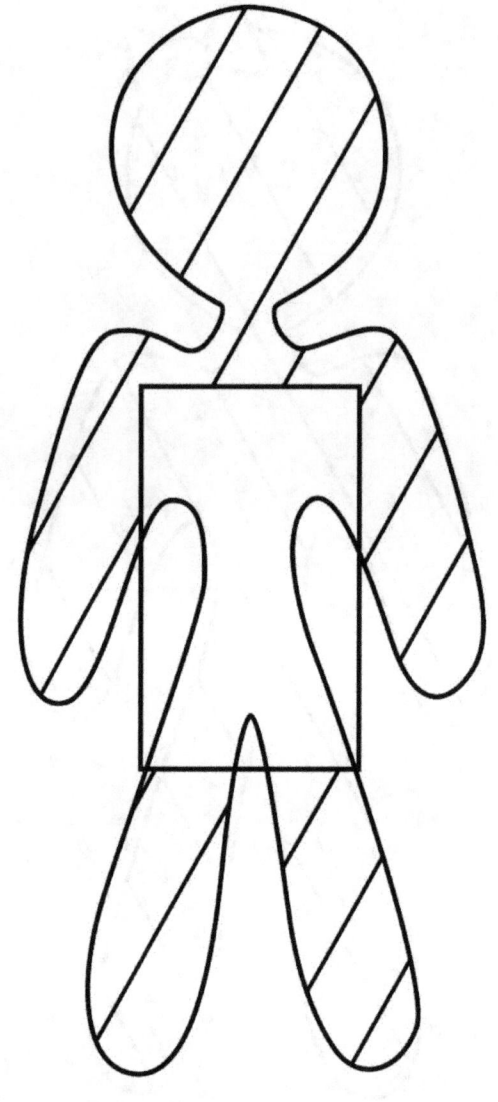

No one should touch you, inappropriately!

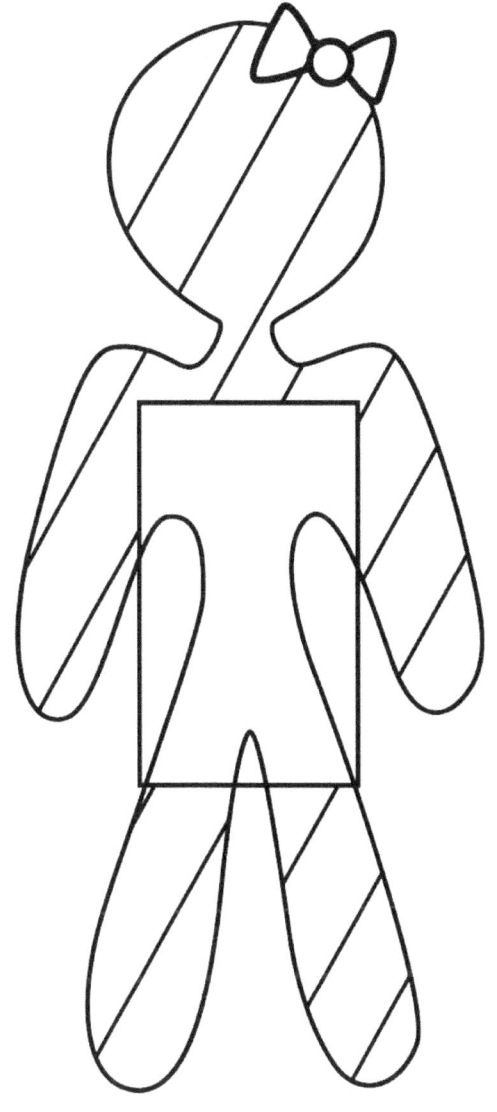

Whether they are your age or older,
Whether they are a family member or a close friend,
And especially, not a stranger!

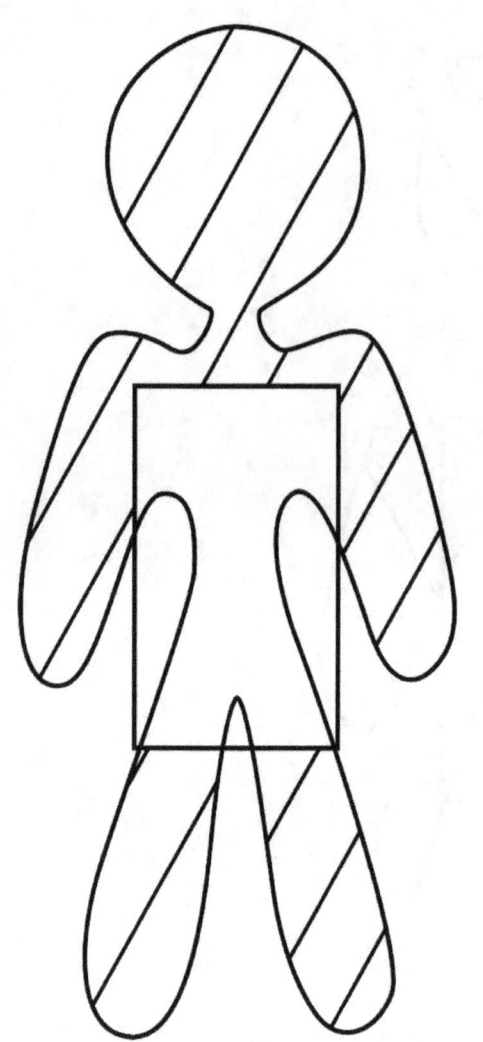
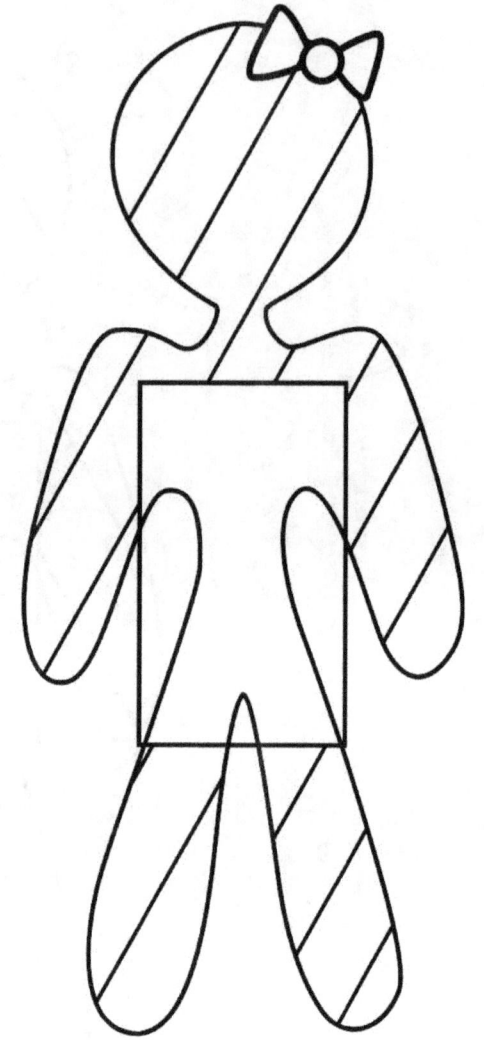

If anyone touches you inappropriately,

Tell
Yell
Scream!

(Don't keep it to yourself)

When we go for walks, you can hold my hand.
When you read to me, you can sit next to me.
When I take a bath, you can hand me my towel.
When I'm playing outside, please keep your eyes on me…
And help keep me safe.

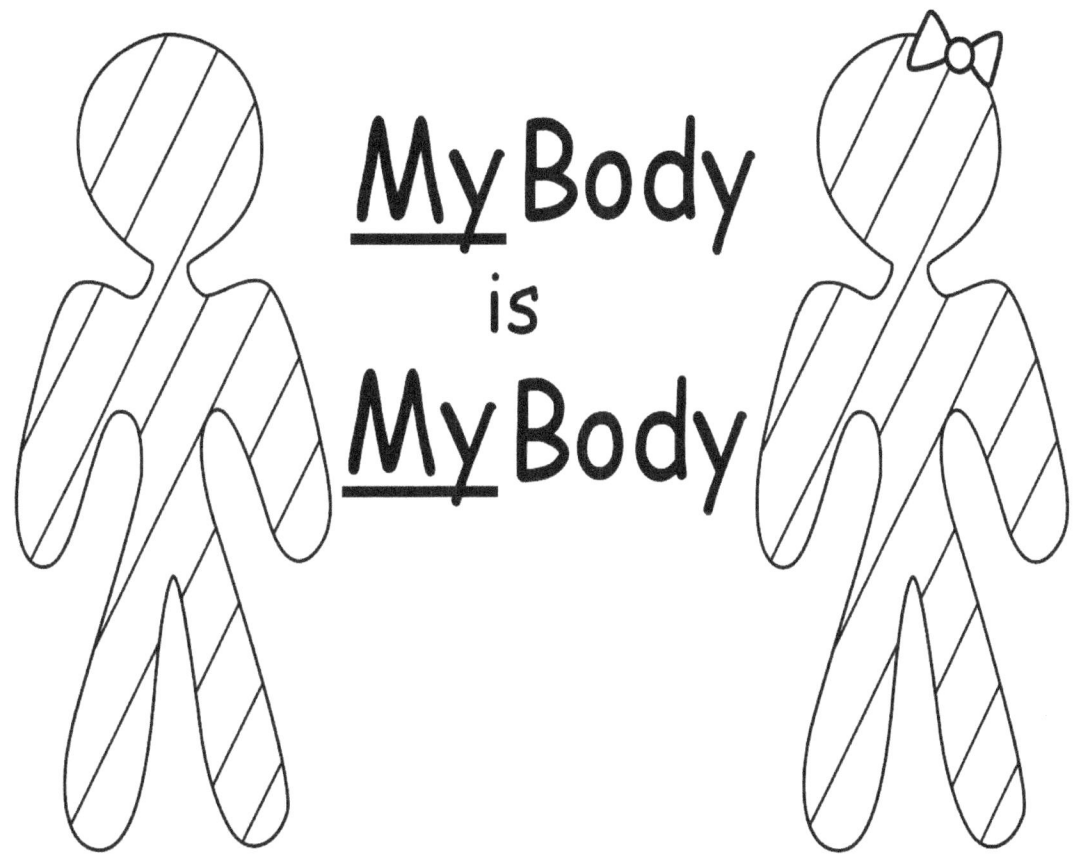

www.ingramcontent.com/pod-product-compliance
Lightning Source LLC
Chambersburg PA
CBHW082249300426
44110CB00039B/2489